# The Wisdom
of
# Catherine,
# the Princess of Wales

© Knightsbridge Publishing
2022

The Wisdom
of
Catherine, the Princess of Wales

Copyright © Knightsbridge Publishing Group

All rights reserved.
No part of this book may be used or reproduced by any means,
graphic, electronic, or mechanical, including photocopying,
recording, taping or by any information storage retrieval system
without the written permission of the publisher except in the
case of brief quotations embodied in critical
articles and reviews.

business@knightsbridgepublishing.com

ISBN: 978-0-9810511-9-2

The quotations included in this book have been gathered
via multiple digital sources
and researched for authenticity and accuracy. Some
quotes collected are being presented without
context, and may therefore be imperfectly worded or attributed.
To the subject and original sources, our thanks, and where
appropriate, our apologies. – The Editor

Printed in the United States of America & United Kingdom

"

I'm still very much Kate.

"

A child's mental health is just as important as their physical health.

"

It is our duty, as parents
and as teachers, to give
all children the space to
build their emotional strength
and provide a strong foundation
for their future.

"

By far the best dressing up outfit I ever had was a wonderful pair of clown dungarees, which my Granny made.

"

No, I had the Levis guy on my wall, not a picture of William, sorry.

"

All of us know someone who has been through difficult emotional times, and we know how hard it can be to see a way forward.

"

We have heard time and time again in the course of our work how talking can help heal the hidden challenges we can't deal with alone.

"

I was quite nervous about meeting William's father, but he was very, very welcoming, very friendly, it couldn't have gone easier really for me.

"

Parents, teachers, and other school staff need the tools to help these young people early in their lives. And the earlier, the better. It is proven that early action prevents problems later in life.

"

Nothing brings me more happiness than trying to help the most vulnerable people in society. It is a goal and an essential part of my life.

"

The Queen, she was really thrilled that it was a little girl, and I think as soon as we came back here to Kensington, she was one of our first visitors here. She always leaves a little gift or something in their room. That just shows, I think, her love for her family.

> Nothing can really prepare you for the sheer overwhelming experience of what it means to become a mother. It is full of complex emotions of joy, exhaustion, love and worry, all mixed together.

"

William and I feel that every child deserves to be supported through difficult times in their lives.

"

A child who has overcome challenges with proper emotional support will emerge stronger.

> Not all children have the anchor of a strong family.

"

George loves the T-Rex because it's the noisiest and the scariest.

"

The most memorable engagement for me was an away-day to Leicester. I went without William, so I was rather apprehensive about that . . . . [The Queen] was very supportive. The fact she took the time to make sure that I was happy and looked after for that particular occasion, which probably in everything that she's doing is a very small element, it shows just how caring she is really.

"

My little Louis is just so sweet,
[talking about the queen's passing he said],
'Mummy, don't worry. She's now
with great-grandpa.'

"

No one would feel embarrassed about seeking help for a child if they broke their arm – and we really should be equally ready to support a child coping with emotional difficulties.

"

I can remember being at Sandringham, for the first time, at Christmas. And I was worried about what to give the Queen as her Christmas present. I was thinking, 'Gosh, what should I give her?'. I thought, 'I'll make her something.' Which could have gone horribly wrong. But I decided to make my granny's recipe for chutney.

**"**

Every child deserves to grow up knowing their potential and feeling confident that they won't fall at the first hurdle - that they cope with life's setbacks.

"

You know, over the years,
William has looked after me,
he's treated me very well –
as the loving boyfriend he is,
he is very supportive of me through
the good times and also through
the bad times...

> You go from thinking of yourself as primarily an individual to suddenly being a mother, first and foremost.

"

We need to help young people and their parents understand that it's not a sign of weakness to ask for help.

> Some children are tackling tough times without the support that can help them because the adults in their life are scared to ask.

> My parents taught me about the importance of qualities like kindness, respect and honesty, and I realize how central values like these have been to me throughout my life.

"

Since beginning my work in areas like addiction, for example, I have seen time and time again that the roots of poor mental health in adulthood are almost always present in unresolved childhood challenges.

"

I think if you do go out with someone for quite a long time you do get to know each other very, very well... You go through the good times, you go through the bad times, both personally and within a relationship as well.

> Around a third of parents still worry that they will look like a bad mother or father if their child has a mental health problem. Parenting is hard enough without letting prejudices stop us from asking for the help we need for ourselves and our children.

> A huge amount still needs to be done. At the moment hundreds of children are still malnourished

> It is right to talk about motherhood as a wonderful thing, but we also need to talk about its stresses and strains. It's OK not to find it easy, and asking for help should not be seen as a sign of weakness.

"

[The Queen has] been very generous and not sort of being forceful at all in any of her views. I feel she's been sort of a gentle guidance, really, for me.

"

Being able to go into Wimbledon and be part of an amazing atmosphere is special.

"

Personally, becoming a mother has been such a rewarding and wonderful experience. However, at times it has also been a huge challenge. Even for me who has support at home that most mothers do not.

> First-class delivery of children's palliative care is life-changing. When families are confronted with the shattering news that their children have a life-limiting condition, their world can fall apart.

"

Imagine if everyone was able to help just one child who needs to be listened to, needs to be respected, and needs to be loved - we could make such a huge difference for an entire generation.

# Knightsbridge
# Publishing
# Group

© Knightsbridge Publishing
2022

www.ingramcontent.com/pod-product-compliance
Lightning Source LLC
Chambersburg PA
CBHW062114290426
44110CB00023B/2811